The Golden Rules: Following the Common Thread

By Lura Jackson, M.A. Peace and Reconciliation

To Caitlin,
With enduring love & light.
—Lura   June 2025

The Golden Rules: Following the Common Thread. Copyright 2025 by Lura Jackson.

All rights reserved. No part of this publication may be copied, reproduced in any format, by any means, electronic or otherwise, without prior consent from the copyright owner.

Table of Content

Introduction	1
Chapter 1	3
African	5
Australian Aboriginal	7
Indigenous American	9
Egyptian	11
Jain	13
Hindu	15
Ancient Greek	17
Chapter 2	19
Zoroastrian	21
Judaism	23
Buddhist	25
Confucian	27
Daoism	29
Shinto	31
Christian	33
Islam	35
Chapter 3	37
Incan	39
Sikh	41
Latter Day Saints	43
Baha'i	45
Modern Humanist	47
Wiccan	49
Unitarian Universalist	51
Conclusion	53
Bibliography and additional resources	57
Acknowledgements	58
About the author	59

There are creeds and rules to guide us
And help us in life's school,
But the finest creed for every need,
Is the good old golden rule.
(Folk rhyme)

Introduction

Across our long history, countless civilizations of humans have lived upon the Earth. The breadth of our development and the complexities of individual cultures that have existed is mostly lost to us today; we know what we know from the written, oral, and archeological records that remain, and nothing more.

Our written volumes hold a mere 5,000 years of our story; aside from those etched into stone or preserved by fortune, most have been produced in the past two centuries. Archeological records give us evidence of where we were and how we lived, but geological forces and urban development can render such records scant. Our oldest cultural resource as a species is our oral history, but that changes and can become lost over time as native speakers die out or are assimilated. Our history is a skeleton, a framework, mostly missing in flesh and detail.

Suffice to say that many different humans have lived many different lives during the course of our species' existence. Some have lived nobly, some have been cruel. Some have suffered terribly and endured great loss. Others have had the privilege of having their basic needs met day in and day out, whether it was while living in birch bark teepees and drawing fish from streams or while dwelling in an earthen hut feasting on figs.

We have lived in so many different places. We have spoken so many different languages. We have worshipped so many gods.

Out of all this, what do we have in common? What, beyond the essentials of breathing air, drinking water, and eating food, have we all shared?

One commonality emerges. Beyond just an idea, or a type of tool, or the shape of a building – this commonality is woven in to the fabric of virtually every human civilization across our planet. It is a constant, universal theme.

That fundamental commonality that exists across so much time and space, that theme of humanity, is a core message of reciprocity. If you wish to do well, begin by helping others around you do well. If you wish to avoid suffering, don't inflict suffering on others. Known as the Golden Rule, versions of it can be found in every religion and philosophy that we still remember.

By looking at this choice pearl – by holding it aloft it in the light – we see ourselves, not only in reflection, but as interconnected beings who want to do well by one another. We have repeatedly discovered the Golden Rule as being key to the formula of a successful and happy life. That's been true for humanity no matter where or when we have lived, as we will illustrate in the coming pages.

In each case, the development of the Golden Rule is unique to the culture that birthed it. At times, it emerges out of an understanding of relationship with the environment and the social importance of community. In other cases, it's brought forth by spiritual and philosophical leaders seeking to share a better way of life with their followers. Regardless of when and how it appears, however, the core principal remains the same.

With that said, let's follow the thread, starting with our oldest memories.

Chapter 1

Our first home as a species was Africa; there, among the abundant forests and savannah, *Homo sapiens* developed approximately 320,000 years ago. For a staggering breadth of time, our families and tribal groups lived together and apart on the great continent, and it is from there that all of our genetic lineage comes.

Modern humans weren't the only hominins to live in Africa, and in fact we first lived alongside the Neanderthals, with whom we shared a common ancestor (*Homo heidelbergensis*). As a species, modern humans are exactly that – modern – with precursor humans living in Africa for six million years or longer.

Unlike our earlier counterparts, modern humans have brains that are physiologically reordered during childhood to improve cognitive thinking. In other words, when humanity developed, we came ready to solve problems.

And there were many problems to solve. The Africa of a quarter million years ago was rife with wildlife, including some of the most dangerous predators we've met as a species. To meet the task, and to provide ourselves with food and shelter, humanity began to innovate.

For the most part, early humans kept to small family groups, harvesting different foods and hunting various animals depending on where and when we lived. In South Africa 160,000 years ago, for example, we roasted and ate gigantic land snails as big as our hands and slept on hay bedding. Around the continent, we cooked and ate starchy root plants and collected fruits like cantaloupe, pears, and watermelon. Ground nuts were harvested and processed for protein and fiber.

The abundance of Africa, paired with constant threats from predators, disease, and a challenging climate, kept our ancestors constantly on the move. Rather than settling down in any particular place, they moved into regions when conditions were favorable, and then moved out when resources dwindled. This theme of nomadism characterized most of our time as a species.

By necessity, our communities were egalitarian in our early years. It was critically important for humans to coexist with one another within their groups, otherwise division could result – leading to the group's overall weakening and the individual's potential demise. As such, early humans developed as nomadic hunter gatherers who were rooted in social cohesion reinforced by customs designed to promote harmony. This need to preserve our small social groups laid the bedrock for the Golden Rule.

It wasn't until approximately 194,000 years ago that modern humans actively left Africa for the first time, interbreeding with other human species (including Neanderthals and Denisovans, who had left the continent around 100,000 years earlier) as they did so.

Within a relatively short timeframe, humanity spread to whole new lands, crossing the vast steppes of what would become Eurasia, sailing across oceans with seemingly endless horizons, and launching the foundations of today's cultures.

African - 120,000 years ago

> *"If you do not allow your neighbor to reach nine you will never reach ten."* – Akan saying

Humans in Africa – whether dwelling on the savannah, in rainforests, or in deserts – developed myriad distinct cultures, and that diversity led to curiosity. Approximately 120,000 years ago, bands of humans from across the continent were engaging in trade and interacting with one another for a variety of purposes.

As one would expect from hundreds of thousands of years of intertwined existence, there is not a uniform culture or belief system that succinctly encapsulates humanity's development in Africa. There are, however, commonalities across the continent that indicate the most enduring and important beliefs among the African peoples that comprise human ancestry and modern African cultures.

Perhaps the best representation of indigenous African spiritual beliefs is the concept of Ubuntu. As a philosophy, it teaches "I am what I am because of who we all are," reminding those who embrace it of the importance and necessity of growing together and recognizing the truth of shared fate.

Roughly translated as "humanity toward others," ubuntu is a rich philosophy that encompasses values such as sharing, being respectful, and prioritizing the preservation of life above all else. Rather than glorifying individual enlightenment, ubuntu instead emphasizes community enrichment. As such, whenever someone is acting for the greater good of their family, band, or tribe, they are engaging in a form of mutual empowerment that elevates everyone involved.

Ubuntu has been a part of the culture of African tribes going back to the earliest days, according to the oral history of the Bantu, Zulu, and Xhola tribes. The San people, the oldest continuously existing tribe in Africa at 20,000 years old, have been recognized as today's longest ongoing practitioners of the ubuntu philosophy. While the manifestation of ubuntu can vary from one region to another, reciprocity is at its core.

To the Shona people of Zimbabwe, for example, ubuntu is encapsulated in the phrase *munhu munhu muvanhu*, or "a person is a person through other persons." In this, we can understand that our very humanity is gained when we assist one another – and without it, without that process of reflection and action and reflection, we aren't fully realized as individuals. The popular saying *Mwana anorerwa nemusha kana kuti nedunhu*, or "It takes a clan, village or community to raise a child," is another piece of wisdom from the Shona people.

Outside of its teachings of communal reciprocity, ubuntu orders the world spiritually and philosophically into three layers, recognizing the sphere of humans and living beings in one, spirits in another, and a supreme being known as *Musikavanhu/Nyadenga/unkulunkulu*, or the God of Creation, into the third. It is from communing with the latter layers that the moral standards of ubuntu are derived.

Australian Aboriginal - 60,000 years ago

"Our identity with land is sacred and unique. We have a very strong sense of community. All persons matter. All of us belong." – Miriam-Rose Ungunmerr, Dadirri

Leaving Africa alongside the first migrating humans, and mixing briefly with the Neanderthals along with other contemporary human populations, the Aborigines provide us with the oldest genetic ancestry for all modern humanity (outside of the Africa-based populations that did not migrate). Some scientists believe the Aborigines arrived in Australia as early as 120,000 years ago, although archeological evidence doesn't yet support that claim.

The Aborigines found their new homeland to be a difficult place to survive; they originally adhered to the east and west coasts and relied on coastal resources for food. Over time, existence in the hot desert environment became easier, though they were quick to migrate from a settlement if it became too arid and water became scarce. Living in small family groups, they were semi-nomadic and followed seasonal cycles to take advantage of the best food and climate conditions.

The Aborigines fashioned homes out of rock shelters and harvested wild seeds that were then ground down into flour. They ate fruits and plants, including wild passionfruit, oranges, bush tomatoes and bush bananas. They made pigments for their skin and clothes and combined them with mica to make a reflective paint for artwork. Edge-ground hatchets were used to cut trees and butcher animals.

For 20,000 years, the Aborigines lived alongside and hunted megafauna, including the giant flightless bird

Genyornis, the 12-foot tall and wombat-like *Diprotodon*, the marsupial lion, and the marsupial tapir. Living with animals of all sizes and following the signs of the land to know when to migrate contributed to a deep sense of interconnection with the land and its inhabitants. Like Indigenous peoples around the world, this understanding manifests in a philosophy of reciprocity in relation to one's surroundings and a deep sense of belonging to place and community.

Aboriginal spirituality goes beyond recognizing the equality inherent to living beings and grants equivalent respect to inanimate but critically supportive features of the land itself. During Dreamtime, or the time period the Aboriginal people refer to as the beginning of creation, the Spirits made everything in existence before disappearing. Some of these Spirit ancestors went into the rocks and water and dirt, and so all of these elements are considered sacred alongside their living counterparts.

Importantly, Aborigines view the Dreamtime as continually happening – meaning the acts of creation, of imbuement, and of shared existence alongside Spirit ancestors – are continually unfolding in the living world around us. That philosophy, in part, is what guides the Aboriginal understanding of reciprocity and connection with all elements around us.

Indigenous American - 28,000 B.C.

"Respect for all life is the foundation." – The Great Law of Peace

Ever venturous, humans did not stop when they reached the edge of the Eurasian supercontinent. Instead, whether by water or by land bridge, we found our way to a place as-yet untouched by human habitation. Traveling south, north, inland and eastward as the Laurentide Ice Sheet receded, humanity gradually explored the continent that would come to be called North America.

Along the way, some populations opted to stop in particularly favorable locations, choosing to dedicate themselves and their subsequent generations to hunting seals, buffalo, deer, or fish. Over time, they became tribes defined by their language, their prey, and their crafting materials.

In the Southwestern part of today's United States, for example, the ancestral Pueblos settled in the arid land to farm corn. They created complex irrigation systems that enabled them to farm beans and squash (with the three crops becoming known as the "Three Sisters" for how well they support one another and Native communities as a whole). Women learned to make ceramic pots and woven baskets to collect and contain the harvest. They lived in permanent stone and mud structures with thatched roofs that were arranged in villages.

In the Northeast, by contrast, the Wabanaki people developed their lives around coastal fishing and hunting. Along with gathering shellfish and spearing pollock, they learned to hunt massive whales as readily as the great moose and caribou wandering the land. Wild berries, nut butters, and maple syrup flavored their dishes, while fiddleheads, dandelion greens, and seaweed provided additional nutrition. Their homes were birch bark teepees and lodges.

While the people who settled in North America developed in unique ways depending on where they called home – culminating in an astounding 500 distinct languages at time of European contact – they were joined by a similar belief in interconnection. Tribes traded widely from one end of the continent to the other, relying on complex waterways that served as arteries of life.

The prevalence of the understanding of ecological interconnection can be gleaned from the oral history of Native Americans. In Wabanaki legend, the tribe originated when their hero-creator, Glooskap, shot an arrow into an ash tree and they came tumbling out. Both ash and birch trees became indispensable parts of Wabanaki culture, lending to the creation of everything from hunting gear to canoes to baskets. Caring for these resources – along with all other sources of food, shelter, and life – became a primary function of the tribe.

These values were embodied by the Great Law of Peace of the Iroquois Confederacy, being one of the world's oldest participatory democracies. Indigenous American communities were typically ruled by consensus, meaning decisions were made as a group. During times of crisis, leaders were appointed, but these usually weren't fixed positions. Men and women were viewed as equals and both could hold leadership roles.

Egyptian - 8000 B.C.

> *"Do for one who may do for you, that you may cause him thus to do."* – The Tale of the Eloquent Peasant, 109-110

Unlike most of the African continent, which saw humans following the patterns of flora and fauna and sheltering from seasonal weather patterns, the area that would become Egypt was different. The seasonal flooding of the Nile River turned the otherwise brown desert green, opening the opportunity for a new era in humanity's development. Here, we found, we could stay in one location – but it would require the careful and thoughtful management of seeds and water.

And so humanity developed agriculture, fostering a new relationship with plants and farm animals and, for the first time, becoming fully sedentary. Egyptian peoples, one of the first to settle down, did so around 10,000 years ago.

Wheat was an essential part of this transition, as it grew favorably in the Nile's rich floodplains. Wheat and barley were used for bread and beer, staples in the diet of early Egyptians, and fish was incorporated when possible. Cows were domesticated 5,000 years ago in the region, providing milk and beef, while vegetables such as onions, radishes, garlic, and salad greens supplemented the diet.

Over time, small villages formed, occasionally consolidating into cities of thousands of people. One such city, Nekhen, arose 7,000 years ago to become the home of the Cult of Horus; it served as the capital of the region for 2,000 years. Its rival, Abydos, became dominant afterward; it was the home of worship for Isis and Osiris.

Approximately 4,500 years ago, the pyramids of Giza and Saqqara were built, demonstrating humanity's capacity for organizing and building enormous structures for the first time – along with their belief in life after death. Egypt's cultural influence was strong, and its pantheon of gods and goddesses held sway in North Africa for thousands of years.

One goddess in particular, Ma'at, was the patron of Truth, Balance, Order, Harmony, Reciprocity, Propriety, and Justice (considered the Seven Principles of Ma'at). Everyone was expected to abide by these principals in their daily interactions, particularly if they held a position of power over someone else.

The societies of ancient Egypt were matrilineal, a characteristic largely influenced by their interpretation of "as above, so below" – with Isis representing the dominant sun and Osiris the moon. That relationship evolved into Egypt's matrilineal structure, which granted queens the most power, including the power to crown the king or beget the next pharaoh. Women were free to purchase property, own businesses, get divorced, travel, and speak on their own behalf in court.

From within this egalitarian culture comes a version of the Golden Rule, as spelled out in the *Tale of the Eloquent Peasant*, a nearly 4,000-year-old Egyptian text reflecting on ethical order.

Jain - 3000 B.C.

> *"In happiness and suffering, in joy and grief, we should regard all creatures as we regard our own self."* – Lord Mahavir 24th Tirthankara

One of the oldest religions in the world, Jainism has deep roots in Northern India. Its name comes from the Sanskrit word *Ji*, which means to conquer, as those who follow its path battle against their earthly passions and bodily form to attain omniscience.

Believed to predate the arrival of Indo-Aryan settlers and the Indus Valley civilization, Jainism's origins resonate with some of the earliest known beliefs of humanity. Like the Australian Aborigines, Jainists honor the living essence of all objects, whether animate or inanimate, and subscribe fully to a belief in immutable interconnection. This foundation would have served early followers well after arriving in Northern India amidst the subtropical climate and vibrant ecosystem.

By 9000 B.C., humans were cultivating agriculture in India, growing wheat and barley in fields that were fertilized by sheep and goats. A few thousand years later, cattle were domesticated in the region, further lessening the early Indians' dependence on hunting and solidifying the transition away from their nomadic lifestyle. Pumpkin, peas, brinjal (eggplant) and spinach soon became regular agriculture staples, while an abundance of wild fruit – including mangoes, bananas, papayas, melon, and more – provided ample flavor to any given dish.

During millennia of learning to exist alongside a rich tapestry of life, the humans who came to call India home planted the seeds of Jainism that would inform their understanding of the world around them.

Key to the more than 5,000-year history of Jainism is nonviolence, encapsulated in the phrase "*Ahimsa Paramo Dharmah.*" Ahimsa means nonviolence, paramo means topmost, and dharmah translates to ultimate; together it illustrates how nothing is more important than following and embodying nonviolence.

Jain monks and nuns have been known to exemplify this creed by taking painstaking effort to remove insects and other organisms from their path before they walk, sit, or lay down. Further, they commonly wear masks to prevent accidentally inhaling microbes that wouldn't survive in the human body.

Modern Jainism was formally founded by Mahavir, born in 599 B.C. in Patna, one of the India's oldest cities. A member of the warrior class by birth, Mahavir fully embraced the ancient teachings of ahimsa that resonated in the quiet pathways of the old city.

Mahavir embodied his beliefs in every regard; he wore no clothing and ate only the bare minimum needed to survive – until he opted to stop doing so and starved to death at the age of 72.

Before his passing, Mahavir expanded upon and outlined the principles of Jainism beyond ahimsa, adding *anekantvada* (holding a multiplicity of views), *aparigraha* (non-possessiveness), to never steal, and *brahmacharya* (renouncing sex and marriage).

Hindu - 2000 B.C.

> *"This is the sum of duty. Do not unto others that which would cause you pain if done to you."* – *Mahabharata* 5, 1517

In the hot and arid climate of what is today Pakistan, the Indus River Valley provided fertile ground for the development of Hinduism, creating what would eventually become the third largest religion in the world.

Early settlements in the valley were augmented with a variety of livestock such as cattle, goats, pigs, and chicken. With sparse natural vegetation, meat provided the lion's share of the daily diet, along with dairy products, fish, and shellfish. Wheat and barley were the primary crops grown in the valley, while lentils and similar pulses (such as peas) were grown for added nutrition.

The dry climate and soil were offset by the region's periodic monsoons, serving to replenish the valley's soils and rivers. While the monsoons weren't always consistent, residents learned to adapt by shifting to drought-resistant crops such as rice when needed.

Dwellings were mud-brick houses that typically had their own hearths with tandoori-style ovens, giving the opportunity for residents to easily bake bread and meats for their families. Within a few millennia, towns and cities formed, providing the opportunity for Hinduism to blossom amid busy streets characterized by town squares, sewer systems, granaries, and public baths.

Rather than coming from a single root, Hinduism is a joining of many threads, languages, and beliefs, all of which were brought to the Indus valley by settlers, traders, and travelers. Despite this splintered origin, it gained cohesion in its commonalities.

Most practitioners of Hinduism base their beliefs on ancient scriptures called the Vedas, with additional texts (such as the Upanishads and Ramayana) providing their own nuances of understanding. Hindus also embrace following dharma, defined broadly as the cosmic order that governs everything in existence – and more narrowly as a personal compass that guides actions and informs behavior.

Early on, women and men were treated equally. Both sexes participated in the economy and made significant decisions of their own accord, both participated in religious ceremonies, and both could remarry without issue (although these privileges changed gradually over time as women's rights eroded). Child marriages were effectively nonexistent.

There is no evidence that kings, queens, pharaohs, or other such hereditary rulers held sway in the Indus valley. Instead, it is believed that residents were governed either by elected officials or appointed elites.

The Mahabharata, being an epic tale that helped shaped belief during the transition to sectarian Hinduism around 400 B.C., provides the clearest and most familiar rendition of the Golden Rule that we've explored so far. With its reference to duty, it immediately evokes dharma, making it clear that humans are cosmically bound to behave with reciprocity in mind.

Ancient Greek - 1200 B.C.

> *"Do not do to others that which angers you when they do it to you...Expect to fare well or ill according as you are disposed well or ill toward me."* – Isocrates, "Nicocles," 3.61

Around the brilliance of the Mediterranean sea, a new civilization formed in the remains of the Mycenean empire, gathering its people and its wits from across the region. The Mediterranean climate was ideal for growing wheat, barley, olives, figs, pears, pomegranates, and vegetables, fueling the rise of exports that, in turn, enabled the import of new goods.

The ancient Greeks kept small herds of sheep, goat, and the occasional cow for cheese, leather, and wool. Their houses were made from mud bricks and wood, and were typically two stories high. They included amenities such as shutters to block out the hot sun and a courtyard for relaxation.

Like the Myceneans, the Greeks were familiar with bronze working, creating art, and organizing cities, and by 1000 B.C., the first polis (city) was formed. With its formation, Greeks became bound to the rule of common laws within their respective city-states. Different poleis maintained different ways of life, as determined by the traditions of their constituents. As such, there was dramatic difference in how ancient Greeks lived based on their city-state of residence.

In inland Sparta, for instance, boys went into military service at the age of 7, training and living in encampments until the age of 26 and undergoing drills through the age of 60. Spartan women also engaged in physical training, but rather than strengthening their bodies for war, they were strengthening them for child birth. Notably, Spartan women were among the best educated in Greece; they owned and managed property and kept business flowing whenever Spartan men were engaged in war.

Located on the coast, Athens was a distinct opposite. It embraced art, personal freedom, and democracy; it was here that the Greek culture of philosophy thrived. Despite this, Athenian women were much less liberated than their Spartan counterparts; as second-class citizens, they couldn't vote, hold property, or serve in government.

In common practice, ancient Greeks were guided by such concepts as *xenia*, loosely translated as guest-friendship. In following it, a stranger could come to any house and receive food and a bath before the host would even ask his name. Effectively, *xenia* is a form of communal reciprocity.

Greek thinkers, meanwhile, pondered the cosmological order of the universe, including Thales of Miletus, who asserted that water is the *archê*, or originating source, of all bodies. Along with this unifying concept, he maintained that everything (animate or otherwise) had a soul.

This rich mixture of tradition and cultures combined to create ancient Greek philosophy, from which our example derives. Living in Athens around 400 B.C., Isocrates wrote "Nicocles" using the voice of his titular former student (who became king of Cyprus); it provides instruction on how to live well and fairly.

Chapter 2

At this point, we've covered hundreds of thousands of years of human history, leaping across our earliest ancestors and diving into the relatively young cultures that emerged from those near-primordial beginnings. In our oldest cultures – those of Africa and indigenous peoples in Australia and the Americas – we see common themes of interconnection, serving to create irrevocable foundations of reciprocity that continue to inform modern members of those cultures as well as our global community as a whole.

But that, as they say, is just the beginning. As we have already seen in the development of Egyptian and Greek cultures, and in the diversity emerging from the Indus Valley, humans are uniquely gifted with creating myths to help explain the natural world and enforce societal order.

That doesn't mean, of course, that all human myths are based in good – or even reciprocal – intentions. More often than not we can find examples of how religion was created or warped to suit enacting misdeeds upon others. Indeed, our history books are filled with examples of cruel empires, stratified societies, and suffering individuals, regardless of whether or not they come from cultures that manifested a Golden Rule or not.

Of course, the existence of a Golden Rule – as with any religion or ethical code – is independent of how it is embodied, whether by its followers or the wider culture as a whole. With that said, we will continue our observation of humanity as it continues to travel the long path of time, arriving again and again at a familiar well to draw up a drop of distilled wisdom for the furtherance of its enlightenment.

The next 1,200 years of humanity's story contain the emergence of multiple Golden Rules, along with some of the most influential religions the world had yet seen. Several arose within a few hundred years of one another as a combination of political and social unrest fueled the holy fire of spiritual leaders seeking to show their followers the way to earthly and heavenly bliss.

During this timeframe, the world was becoming a much more connected place. Trade routes snaked across Eurasia and exchanged goods between the bountiful coasts and inland gardens. Rather than enforcing their rule through conquest and military might alone, empires found that they needed to develop new systems of fairer management and governance to effectively maintain their power.

This combination of trade and empires based on assimilation rather than conquest favored the spread of Golden Rules and their associated spiritual teachings as new populations became exposed for the first time. In some situations, the overbearing presence of empires prompted the development of countering spiritual philosophies, some of which outlasted the empires they challenged.

Technological innovation also played a hand in enabling the Golden Rules to proliferate, from the building of vast road systems and improvements in pack animal transport to new ways in maritime travel that enabled direct trade between Africa and Asia.

One by one, Golden Rules were surmised and expressed in pockets across the rapidly developing world, gradually illuminating their cultures as they did so.

Zoroastrian - 600 B.C.

> *"That nature alone is good which refrains from doing unto another whatsoever is not good for itself."* –
> Dadisten-I-dinik, 94,5

Far from the civilized realm of western Asia, before Cyrus unified Persia, the priest Zoroaster (also known as Zarathustra) developed a new understanding of religion that incorporated a supreme god, seeing the world as a dichotomy of good and evil (including foretelling an apocalyptic battle in which the victorious forces of good would restore it to its once-perfect state), and the behavior-dependent possibility of going to heaven after death.

In the time of Zoroaster, the arid plateau of what would become Iran hosted a collection of semi-nomadic tribes who tended to herds of sheep, goats, and cattle. The daily diet nearly always included multiple meals of rice, sometimes served with nuts such as almonds or pistachios, or accented with fruits, including raisins, apples, figs, and apricots. While most dishes were vegetarian, meat (in the form of stews or kebabs) was occasionally consumed. Saffron, being the most expensive spice in the world today, was grown and cultivated in the region as far back as 1000 B.C. For early Persians, it was one of many spices that balanced the flavors of their meals.

Dwellings in Iran varied between the north and the south, based on the availability of materials. In the south, homes were typically domes made from clay; in the north, they were built from rocks carved into blocks.

Zoroaster is believed to have been born in the northeastern part of Persia, most likely into a tribe that worshipped a multitude of deities that were not dissimilar to those found in Hinduism. According to legend, he experienced a vision of a divine being at the age of 30 while participating in a ritual. It would set the stage for him to formulate the worship of the being, which he named Ahura Mazda.

With a belief in judgement-after-death, Zoroaster proscribed good behavior to his followers, asserting that to behave fairly and mindfully would result in ascension to heaven. Humans were regarded as equals by Zoroaster regardless of their sex or background. Animals were treated somewhat differently, as he believed they were divided into good and evil categories, with the former (cows and dogs, mainly) being treated with reverence and the latter (frogs, snakes, scorpions, insects, and so on) being exterminated whenever found.

Following the rise of Zoroaster, Cyrus the Great dramatically expanded the power and renown of Persia to the point that half of the world's population fell within it, effectively connecting Africa, Asia, and Europe together for the first time through a vast network of roads. This system, in part, allowed the spread of the beliefs of Zoroastrianism, which proved to be significantly influential to the major religions of today.

Judaism - 600 B.C.

> *"What is hateful to you, do not to your fellow man. This is the law: all the rest is commentary."* – Talmud, Shabbat 31a

On the eastern edge of the Mediterranean Sea, the ancient Hebrews maintained a shared culture based in common myths, rituals, and history going back to at least 1000 B.C. Key to the development of the Jewish faith was belief in YHWH ("Yahweh"), an all-powerful god. As such, Judaism was one of the first fully monotheistic faiths.

Descendants of the kingdoms of Israel and Judah would go on to formally found the modern day version of Judaism in 600 B.C. by writing down their shared beliefs and specific practices in a collection of five books known as the Torah.

Nomadism was a defining characteristic of the early followers of Judaism, as they tended to sheep and goats and led their herds to favorable places. In Canaan, they settled into sedentary life, adopting agriculture and sometimes forming cities.

The daily diet was centered around wheat, barley, wine, and olives. One estimate provides that three-quarters of the early Jewish people relied exclusively on bread for their meals of the day. Additional nutrition came from figs, lentils, pistachios, and occasional boiled meat.

Unlike some religions based in agricultural societies, Judaism does not hold a view of animals as being subservient to man. This is illustrated in the Talmud when Rabbi Yehuda HaNasi initially scorns a young calf who runs to him for help to escape the butcher's blade. For thirteen years afterward, he suffered from a painful illness.

Then, one day, a servant was sweeping Rabbi Yehuda's house and came upon a weasel's nest. Proceeding to sweep out the helpless babies, Rabbi Yehuda stopped her with a cry, saying, "God is good to all; Whose compassion are over all God's creatures." His empathy was treated in kind, and Rabbi Yehuda was swiftly cured.

Families were patriarchally-oriented, with males inheriting property and determining the course of the family's path. Women were excluded from participating in most social, economic, and religious activities alongside men, sometimes being given separate areas to conduct their practices or business in.

In cities, Jewish people were able to consider life outside of farming, and some became craftspeople, shopkeepers, and traders. In this fashion, Judaism began to spread slowly throughout the region – a spread that accelerated rapidly as the population experienced multiple diasporas that saw its people traveling to new lands while maintaining their beliefs.

Many of the common practices of modern Judaism, including celebrating Passover, honoring the Sabbath, and ritual bathing, became widespread by 100 B.C. In its entirety, the Judaic religious code advocates for living ethically and in a godly manner, as exemplified by Rabbi Akiba's proclamation in the second century that the Golden Rule is the great principal of the Torah.

Buddhist - 500 B.C.

> *"One should seek for others the happiness one desires for oneself."* – Gautama Buddha

In the northeastern region of India, near the Ganges River basin in today's Nepal, Buddhism blossomed from the wisdom of Gautama Buddha ("the enlightened one").

In 6th century B.C., the basin was a place of constant warfare between the 16 kingdoms that called it home. Against this backdrop of struggle, Siddhartha Gautama was born; per legend, he was a prince raised in luxury who turned his back on his responsibilities of earthly rulership and instead opted to pursue a purely spiritual path.

Buddha and his disciples followed a vast network of trade routes to spread his understanding of enlightenment and "win the deathless state." They traveled throughout the year, pausing only to shelter in winter. Wherever they stopped, they attracted new followers to their faith.

In the time of the Buddha, meals were simple. Breakfast most often consisted of rice porridge made with ample water and a ball of honey, though it might also be made with milk curds, fruit (such as jackfruit, breadfruit, or mango), and meat or fish. Boiled rice was a staple, as were baked grains like wheat, graham flour, millet, and barley. Leafy vegetables were eaten often, along with cucumbers, eggplant, and the occasional lotus root.

Dwellings were typically made of wood. Buddhist monks (who could be men or women) sometimes lived in monastic houses called *viharas*; they were fashioned from rock-cut stone and featured stone beds.

During Buddha's life, the spread of Buddhism was relatively limited owing to a lack of written materials and inscriptions. That changed around 250 B.C. when emperor Ashoka the Great declared Buddhism to be India's official religion, prompting its widespread adoption across the region.

The Golden Rule is clearly present in Buddha's teachings, focusing on the importance of promoting an equivalent level of happiness in others that you yourself would desire. Unlike India's traditional caste system that dictates one's position in society, becoming enlightened is not restricted based on birthright.

According to Buddha's teachings, anyone can become a Buddha regardless of caste or gender, and there will be (and have been) many Buddhas wherever life can be found. Becoming a Buddha involves adopting a realistic viewpoint of the world and one's position in it while also maintaining the perspective that change is fundamental to existence (or, put another way, that nothing is unchanging). This approach of open-ended enlightenment attracted many who saw themselves restricted by societal rules.

One of the core values of Buddhism, *Sila*, further illustrates the depth of belief in equality. It holds that all living entities, regardless of complexity, are to be treated equally under the principal of reciprocity.

Confucian - 500 B.C.

> *"...never impose on others what you would not choose for yourself."* – Confucius, Analects XV.24

On the eastern coast of China, the life and lessons of Confucious served to create guidelines that established widespread education and ethics across the region.

Born to a family with social status, Confucious is said to have held multiple offices in the nearby kingdom of Lu, including Director of Corrections, Foodstuffs Scribe, and Scribe in the Field. Clearly learned and lettered, Confucious maintained high standards that reportedly saw him moving from province to province in search of a suitable ruler to serve.

As he grew older, Confucious moved away from appointed positions, and instead devoted himself to teaching – earning recognition as the first dedicated teacher in China. He focused his efforts on 77 disciples, who in turn trained 3,000 additional students – generating a massive wealth of written materials that contributed to the understanding of Confucianism.

During the time of Confucious, meals tended to include rice, wheat, and millet as their primary grains. Fish and vegetables were important additions, particularly along the coast, while peaches, apricots, and citrons were locally grown fruits. Meat in the form of chicken, pork, and cattle was also consumed, although records indicate that it was mostly men who ate meat.

For his part, Confucious is said to have consumed inexpensive and economical meals, although in his extensive teachings he outlined recommended dishes for multi-course formal meals. Every dish was replete with meaning as, for example, six cold side dishes (including jellyfish salad, spiced duck tongue, and conch jelly) represented the "Six Arts," including archery, calligraphy, mathematics, and music.

The quality of one's dwelling in this time period depended on wealth and social status, with peasants living in huts with bamboo or thatch roofs and merchants living in multi-story wooden homes topped by clay tiles. Timber frames were ubiquitous, as were pounded-earth floors. The homes of wealthier families were designed around courtyards, with the wealthiest families having multiple courtyards to host guests and conduct business.

Rather than creating a religion, Confucious's purpose was to create ethical, moral, and social standards that would lend to an improved society following the decline of the Zhou dynasty. Through his teachings, Confucious aimed to establish peace and order.

Asked what single word could serve as the principle of life, Confucious replied, "Perhaps the word 'reciprocity.'" Confucious outlined that human life is governed by five relationships – between parent and child, minister and ruler, husband and wife, older and younger brother, friend and friend – and in these relationships, reciprocity is key for balance.

Importantly, Confucious believed in equal access to education, meaning that anyone could – and should – engage in higher learning to better themselves and the world around them. Prior to the adoption of Confucianism, only wealthy boys would receive an education.

Daoism - 500 B.C.

> *"Regard your neighbor's gain as your own gain, and your neighbor's loss as your own loss."* – Tai Shang Kan Yin P'ien

Developed simultaneously with Confucianism, Daoism emerged in part as a rejection of Confucian rigidity and instead focused on honing one's ability to interpret and flow with the natural world. Key to Daoism are *wu-wei* (or acting spontaneously, morally and without discrimination), rejecting discursive reasoning, and embracing meditation (described as the fasting of the mind).

Laozi, Daoism's founding figure, is shrouded in mystery, and modern scholars are divided as to whether or not he actually existed. Some contend he was born as Lao Dan in Chu, a state located in the southern Zhou dynasty, where he served the Zhou empire as a great thinker. As the Zhou declined, Lao Dan became frustrated with the people in government who refused to give up corrupt ways of life. He left his position and began wandering the country, emphasizing humility and virtue as he did.

Whether or not Laozi existed, the lessons of Daoism resonated strongly with the people of rural China who encountered them. Daoism's popularity was due in part to its opposing structure to Confucianism, earning it the moniker "the other way." Rather than prescribing specific behaviors, Daoism represented an ancient belief in the sacredness of nature and divination. As such, it offered a more spiritual and mystical path for adherents to live by.

The simplicity of the Dao, as compared to Confuciansm, is illustrated by the length of their respective texts. The *Daodejing*, being the formative text of Daoism, is a single book of poetry 5,000 Chinese characters in length. The sacred texts of Confucianism, by comparison, include between nine and seventeen books.

Even as more and more Chinese were becoming distrustful of organized religions, Daoism offered a return to what was considered to be the natural ways of things, providing sanctuary from divisive sects and social unrest. It was seen as stable, unifying, and immutable, all of which was appealing to people undergoing the fall of a powerful dynasty.

Early followers of Daoism would have based their diets around a holistic philosophy that emphasized a connection between food and spiritual health. Meat and fish were both seen as gateways toward violence that caused its consumers to lose their nature and become impure. Strong flavors – including garlic, onions, leeks, and coriander – were to be avoided as they can disturb the body's energetic balance. Fasting, which sometimes focused only on avoiding grains (a practice known as *bigu*), was often prescribed as a means to achieve transcendence.

In terms of interconnection, Daoism's entire emphasis as a philosophy is on the importance of recognizing and honing one's connection with the natural world. In this, reciprocity between all entities is inherent.

Shinto - 300 B.C.

> *"The heart of the person before you is a mirror. See there your own form."* – Traditional Shinto maxim

First inhabited around 30,000 B.C. by paleolithic peoples who migrated via a land straight from Korea, Japan provided a comfortable and relatively sheltered place for the early hunter gatherers who called it home.

As game became more scarce, technologies such as the bow and arrow and polished agricultural tools were developed, setting the stage for the advancement of the Jōmon and the Yayoi cultures. Birds and wild animals such as rabbits and boar were predominant food sources, while rice, buckwheat, barley, beans, soybeans, burdock, and mint were all cultivated crops enjoyed by early Japanese islanders.

The Jōmon and the Yayoi cultures grew and flourished until about 300 B.C., with the Yayoi people in particular holding precursor beliefs to Shintoism. Most importantly, they venerated *kami*, although the beliefs surrounding them were not as centralized or uniform as they later came to be.

When Buddhism was introduced to Japan in the 6th century A.D., the need arose to distinguish it from the beliefs of the Indigenous Japanese. The term Shinto (meaning "the way of the *kami*") came into wide usage for exactly this purpose, giving its followers a cohesive term for their understanding of the natural world.

Even though Shinto became an official religion at that point, it lacked any kind of scripture or sacred dogmas, instead relying on the passed-down traditions. Over time, Shinto branched into three distinct understandings: Folk

Shinto (comprising ancient ways and beliefs), Shrine Shinto (which joins a connection between religion and state and venerates the Japanese Imperial family), and Sect Shinto (a newer movement consisting of 13 separate sects led by different religious founders).

At the heart of Shinto is an embracing of traditional Japanese beliefs. This emerged fully in the 1800s when the Buddhist shogunate was overthrown and the emperor of Japan was restored as the dominant authority. Recognizing a need to return to earlier ways of thought and validate the emperor's rule, Shinto became embellished with a new myth that involved the emperor's descent from sun goddess Amaterasu Omikami.

When it comes to recognizing interconnection, Shinto's perspective of animism provides that all objects have a degree of life to them. As such, trees, mountains, and rivers all become sacred, along with the wildlife that inhabits natural places. As *kami*, they are revered in a sense as deities, held even higher in perspective than humans.

Despite the imbalance of power between *kami* and humans, their relationship is one of necessary reciprocity. *Kami* share their blessings with humans, who in turn leave offerings and give worship to *kami*.

This emphasis on reciprocity extends into modern Japanese culture itself, where harmony is valued as one of the primary desirable facets of life.

Christian - 30 A.D.

> *"In everything, do to others as you would have them do to you."* – Jesus, Matthew 7:12

Rome's aggressive expansion after 300 B.C., which saw it leaving the Italian peninsula and eventually absorbing most of the communities around the Mediterranean, set the stage for the emergence of Christianity.

Historically, ancient Israel was a land rich with tradition and passionate religious fervor, both of which came into conflict with the Roman empire. As such, when Jesus was born in the village of Nazareth, Judea was a place of chaos, division, and wandering prophets.

One such prophet was Jesus's cousin, John the Baptist, who spoke of the coming of the Messiah. Becoming baptized at the age of 30, Jesus began traveling the countryside to visit homes and synagogues all over Judea to spread the message that the spiritual kingdom is greater than the empires of humanity.

Importantly, the God that Jesus spoke of was the same monotheistic pillar of Israel: YHWH. As such, those familiar with ancient Jewish teachings automatically understood who Jesus was referencing, making it easier for the message of the spiritual kingdom to spread.

Not everyone was receptive to Jesus, particularly as word began to spread that Jesus was the "Son of God." This phrasing, which suggested that Jesus carried YHWH's spark of divinity, was offensive to many who held firm to the embedded spiritual traditions of the region – with Jewish leaders in particular calling it blasphemy. Accordingly, a few years after he began teaching, Jesus was crucified at the order of reluctant Roman officials at the behest of a bevy of Jewish elites.

The people who embraced Jesus's message were often the most downtrodden in society. Some were Jewish, accepting Jesus as the Messiah, while others were Gentiles. All were baptized as part of the process of joining the early Christian faith. This openness, along with the teachings of the Kingdom of God, meant that anyone, regardless of ethnicity, social class, or gender, could become a Christian and receive salvation.

In a society where men said daily prayers thanking God they weren't born women, Jesus made it clear that women should not be treated as inferiors. Women were his disciples and his greatest defenders, and the ones who made the proclamation that he had risen from the dead. In fact, women were the widest adopters of early Christianity, with approximately two-thirds of the faith being women in the second century.

By 350, Christianity was adopted by more than half of the citizens in the Roman empire. Following the efforts of missionaries in the 15th and 16th century, Christianity became the largest religion in the world.

Islam - 610 A.D.

> *"None of you [truly] believes until he wishes for his brother what he wishes for himself."* – Number 13 of Imam Al-Nawawi's Forty Hadiths

Around 8000 B.C., the ample grasslands of Arabia had given way almost entirely to the desert. Those who called the peninsula home became expert farmers of wheat and dates, incorporating ritualistic poems into the planting of the date palms. Cattle, sheep, and goats were all common livestock. They lived in homes made from mud bricks, with dwellings oriented inward to emphasize family communion.

Located between the Byzantine and Persian empires, Arabia was perfectly situated to develop a robust culture of trade. Many wealthy merchants came to call the peninsula home, profiting from a proliferation of spices, camels, and slaves.

It was here, in the town of Mecca, that Muhammad (peace be upon him) was born. Like many Arabian cities, Mecca was a jewel of prosperity thanks to the caravan trade. In the case of Mecca, it was doubly popular as it hosted a shrine to pagan deities that saw many pilgrims voyaging to it.

After Muhammad received his vision and began proselytizing about the almighty rule of a single God – called Allah, being the same almighty God worshipped by Jews and Christians, albeit with slightly different connotations – the leaders of the pantheistic Mecca drove him out. Leaving for Medina to the north, Muhammad continued to spread his message, resulting in the eventual conversion of both Medina and Mecca.

Muhammad continued to administer teachings until his death in 632, after which his followers carried the banner of Islam on a conquest that would claim territory spanning from Iran to Egypt. The Arabian empire provided a solid foundation for Islam to spread from, resulting in its widespread adoption around the world today.

The definition of the word Islam encompasses submission, surrender, and obedience to Allah. Simultaneously, it also means peace – signifying to followers that to attain peace within one's life, one must submit fully to Allah. Loving Allah and loving one's neighbor have been recognized as the twin golden commandments of the faith.

Regardless of socioeconomic background, race, or property ownership, all humans are recognized as having been created by Allah and therefore have inherent spiritual equality. While the sacred text of Islam, the Holy Qur'an, does not espouse the subordination of women, some Islamic cultures do – a point that many modern women Muslim scholars challenge on the basis of passages that clearly speak to the equality between men and women in the eyes of Allah.

Muhammad's approach toward women supports that the original intention of Islam was to treat men and women as equals. An orphan who became the father of four daughters, he cherished the women in his life, including his first wife, Khadijah, who consoled him through the shock and confusion of his first vision. He went on to end the infanticide of small girls and to establish definitive rights for women.

Chapter 3

As we leave the first millennium after the birth of Jesus Christ, the world was preparing to enter a new age. The influence of the religions and philosophies that had come before would prove significant in the cultures that emerged later, serving to not only guide their development, but to shape their Golden Rules.

Just prior to Christ's birth, we saw the simultaneous development of defining transcendent thought in three separate places (India, China, and the West). Whether from the mind of a hermit or wandering thinker in Asia, a prophet in Israel, an ascetic in India, or a philosopher in Greece, the so-called Axial Age represented the a pivotal time when humanity was able to look deeply into itself and challenge the established social order as a result. From these crucial underpinnings the tone of the next millennium would be established.

Whereas the previous two millennia saw the foundations of the Abrahamic faiths built – faiths that now guide 4.4 billion followers around the world, far more than are under the umbrella of any other religious teachings – the next millennium would see them refined and refined again. Branches of Christianity, including Catholicism, Protestantism, and Eastern Orthodoxy, sprouted off from the main teachings, culminating in more than 45,000 denominations over the next thousand years.

Just as the myriad civilizations and cultures that humanity has created have spawned exponentially more with familiar themes, so, too, do religions and philosophies diverge into new understandings. At their core, they carry the heart of their source's teachings, and so the Golden Rule assimilates, mutates, and endures.

Of course, to the average human who woke up in the morning one thousand years ago, the historic developments surrounding their lifetime would have had little weight in daily life. Humans of the second millennium after Christ lived primarily in rural villages, although cities such as Constantinople and Toledo flourished to new heights during this time. Daily concerns were virtually unchanged from those of humans living thousands of years prior – and in many cases, dwellings and amenities had developed little during that time.

That stagnation wouldn't last. Along with the rapid expansion of empires fueled by ever-developing technology, the second millennium brought numerous advancements in the field of agriculture, city building, industry, and warfare. That meant that rather than laboring to grow wheat or rice all day, a larger portion of humanity was now free to explore other trades – potentially even devoting themselves fully to art, science, and philosophy, contributing to the dawn of the Renaissance in the late 1400s.

The Industrial Revolution brought perhaps the greatest changes to the lives of the humans we'll be reading about next, signifying a major shift in lifestyle and contributing to the spread of religious and philosophical texts all over the world. For the first time, humanity could see itself in its virtual entirety – and while some exalted at the view, others recognized the need for more cohesion, prompting the generation of a new set of Golden Rules.

Incan -1200 A.D.

> *"Do not to another what you would not yourself experience."* – Manco Capac

Humans reached the Andean highlands of what would become South America around 11,000 B.C. Located some 8,000 feet above sea level, the highlands are a harsh environment characterized by cold weather, a lack of resources, and a shortage of oxygen, but that didn't stop the people who called it home from thriving. By 2000 B.C., the precursors to the Incas had established a robust agricultural society that cultivated potatoes, maize, and beans. Llamas and alpacas were domesticated and served as pack animals as well as sources of food and clothing.

Several cultures developed in the region, including the Huari, who created the first local model of expansion by conquest – effectively serving as an example for the birth of the Incan empire a few hundred years later. As the Incan empire grew, it assimilated or conquered the other cultures around it, absorbing traditional practices and beliefs as it did.

According to Incan tradition, the empire was founded by a single figure, Manco Capac, although no direct evidence remains of his existence. Though the Inca did have a record keeping system utilizing cords and knots (called *quipu*), no sacred text outlining Manco Capac's beliefs remains.

Even still, the mythology surrounding Manco Capac and his teachings is valuable in the sense that it illustrates the primary principles the Incan people wanted to put forward. More importantly, the Golden Rule attributed to him encapsulates the region's traditionally held belief in *ayni*, or the ongoing cycles of reciprocity.

It was in part through this championing of *ayni* that the Incan empire flourished. Vast networks of trade grew between cities, engineering marvels arose, and a system of diversified agriculture that supported millions of people was developed. While the Inca were no strangers to conflict, the groups they conquered were generally allowed to keep their own local religious ways and rulership intact (provided they recognized the supreme rule of the Sapa Inca, or emperor).

The Incan empire was hierarchal and stratified as such. The Sapa Inca was regarded as an earthly deity, and his subjects were generally forbidden from touching him. A court of nobles engaged in political power struggles, while a bevy of administrators were in charge of day-to-day governance. Inca society was further divided into those who spoke its official language (Quechua) and those who didn't.

With that said, there are markers of belief in equality that persisted throughout the Incan empire. The Sapa Inca was known by another title, *Huaccha Khoyaq*, meaning "Lover and Benefactor of the Poor." It was his role alone to be a magnanimous benefactor to the most impoverished subjects, and many Sapa Inca took it seriously, contributing to the spread of resources across the land in an early form of socialism.

Sikh - 1520 A.D.

> *"As thou deemest thyself, so deem others. Then shalt thou become a partner in heaven."* Kabir's Hymns, Asa 17

In the far north of India, descendants of the Indo-Aryan people lived on the abundant alluvial plain. Here, in what would become Punjab, Guru Nanak was born in 1469. Part of the merchant caste, Nanak worked in a granary until he felt compelled to travel. Raised Hindu, Nanak was soon exposed to Muslim, Santism, and Sufism traditions; each would come to influence the development of Sikhism.

Recognized as a guru for his accumulated wisdom and unique perspective, Nanak espoused teachings about the one Divine Being – a being that all humans are directly connected to by way of a divine spark. As such, all humans are inherently equal.

This equality between humans is fundamental for the Sikh faith. From this perspective, no one – regardless of caste, race, gender, or social power – has more innate capacity to attain transcendence than anyone else. There are no priests or clergy in the Sikh faith, and anyone can become a leader in a Sikh community.

Apart from oneness, the second core message of Sikhism is love. Born from an understanding of shared divinity, practicing divine love is viewed as the ultimate form of embodying the faith in daily life. In essence, this amounts to a robust tradition of service to humanity.

Guru Nanak taught his followers that the key to attaining transcendence is looking deeply into oneself to meditate upon the essence of the Divine Being. All external tools, including rote prayers, temples, scriptures, and idols are distractions that serve to distance followers from a truer understanding of oneness.

Guru Nanak's own experiences with looking deeply into the world and people around him are captured in the thousand-plus hymns he wrote. In this way, he incorporated the tradition of the Sants – a religion of northern India typically comprised of dispossessed, poor, and illiterate people who nonetheless composed hymns evoking divine beauty – into Sikhism. The *Adi Granth*, the religion's sacred text, is composed of nearly 6,000 hymns by Nanak and subsequent Sikh Gurus.

From the perspective of Sikhism, all daily activities offer the potential to connect with the divine, including hard labor, walking, and sharing food. Giving food freely to any and all who are in need is an important tradition in the Sikh custom, particularly as it often involves sharing meals across societal barriers, typically while sitting on the ground.

With love a dominant principle in Sikhism, raised animals are treated with utmost compassion. Many Sikh are vegetarian, but it is not required, and some choose to eat meat (though it must not be ritually slaughtered and should be humanely raised). As animals – along with all creation – are similarly part of the Divine Being, being kind to them is as important as being kind to fellow humans.

Latter Day Saints - 1830

"And let every man esteem his brother as himself, and practice virtue and holiness before me." – Doctrine and Covenants 38:24

With the turn of the 1800s, we find the first religion in our list to be founded in the newly-formed country of America. The Church of Latter Day Saints began with a vision of restoration in the modern connection between humanity and God, with new prophets and apostles continuing to arise, bringing with them fresh revelations that further the beliefs laid out in the Old and New Testaments.

When the United States declared its independence, it did so in a landscape very different from the one the European powers first arrived to. While it was true that much of the country remained unexplored and untamed by colonial powers, cities were cropping up across the northeast. Plantations throughout the south were creating new wealth on the backs of African slaves and white indentured servants. A new class of landowners was developing in distinct contrast to rigidly stratified communities in Europe.

For the average person of the time, daily life was not too different from their European brethren. People lived in wooden houses, ate livestock originally imported from Europe, and grew staple crops like potatoes, beans, and grains. Corn, a crop indigenous to the continent, was grown by nearly every household.

Amid this setting of social and economic flux and familiar homelife, Joseph Smith experienced a vision that guided him to excavate tablets that were buried in a hill close to his New York home. The tablets, once translated, reportedly told the story of early Hebrews that had previously come to America centuries before the birth of Jesus Christ. The tablets became the basis of the Book of Mormon, and a new faith was born.

Smith set out to establish Zion, the Kingdom of God; by his visions he was guided to Jackson County, Missouri. However, the local populace was hostile to the Mormons, leading to Smith and 15,000 followers to move on to Indiana for a second attempt. Once there, suspicion once again met the group, and Smith met his untimely fate in a prison at the hands of a murderous mob.

The young church's new president, Brigham Young, led his followers to Utah, where they continue to worship today under the banner of the Latter Day Saints (LDS).

According to LDS belief, people who are open to God's fullness can effectively become gods themselves, with no division in divinity or potential between any individual person. All people, with few exceptions, will experience glory following their death. With the formation of Zion, Jesus will return and create a celestial kingdom upon the Earth with the righteous being its ordained recipients.

The church's beliefs are replete with Smith's influence, including his emphasis on the inherent goodness of humanity. Men and women are regarded as spiritual equals walking side by side, although women are forbidden from the priesthood and from other societal roles.

Baha'i - 1844

> *"And if thine eyes be turned towards justice, choose thou for thy neighbour that which thou choosest for thyself."* Bahá'u'lláh, Epistle to the Son of the Wolf

Persia once again provided fertile ground for the development of a monumental faith with the founding of Baha'i. It's leader, Bahá'u'lláh, was born to a distinguished family, and committed to his standing as a Divine Teacher wholeheartedly – a distinction that resulted in his near-constant imprisonment at the hands of the Shah of Persia and the Ottoman Emperor until his death in 1892. While imprisoned, Bahá'u'lláh wrote the equivalent of 100 volumes to guide his followers.

Among the chief teachings of Bahá'í is the concept that all of humanity is one. Bahá'u'lláh affirmed this understanding by pointing to the ongoing dissolution of racial, national, and religious barriers that had long stood in the way of humanity's eventual unification.

Bahá'u'lláh actively worked to dissolve these barriers himself, declaring that all religions in the world are derived from a singular, holy source – the one God – and that any practical differences are due to the timeframe and region they originated from. By following any religion, in other words, a person was effectively honoring the absolute divinity.

Perhaps one of the most problematic teachings of Bahá'u'lláh – at least to his devout religious contemporaries – is that past traditions ordained by dead ancestors are not automatically correct. Instead, he implored, people should hone their reasoning to assess traditional understandings to determine if they continue to be suitable to their personal spiritual path.

Similarly, the Bahá'í wield science as deftly as they do religious teachings; science and faith are thought of as two wings from the same bird (without which humanity cannot fly). Along with a robust scientific understanding, Bahá'í followers typically have extensive knowledge of other religions. Accordingly, Bahá'í libraries are replete with texts from virtually every faith.

Equality is paramount to the Bahá'í understanding, with no distinction between men and women and their capability for holiness or leadership, and no lines drawn between races, political adherents, or followers of other religions. There are no priests or individual leaders in Bahá'í communities, which are instead managed by a council of elected leadership.

While there are no dietary restrictions to Bahá'í followers, who can now be found all over the world, the faith impresses the importance of treating animals well, as this passage from Abdu'l-Baha, Bahá'u'lláh eldest son, recounts: "...to blessed animals the utmost kindness must be shown, the more the better. Tenderness and loving-kindness are basic principles of God's heavenly Kingdom."

In writing about the core essence of being a Bahá'í, Abdu'l-Baha puts love and peace at the forefront. "To be a Bahá'í simply means to love all the world; to love humanity and try to serve it; to work for universal peace and universal brotherhood."

Modern Humanist - 1927

> *"According to the fundamental reciprocity principle, each one of us should attempt to treat others as we would have others treat us. The corollary is also true: we should not treat others as we would not like to be treated by them."* – Rodrigue Tremblay, *The Code for Global Ethics: Ten Humanist Principles*

As the world accelerated toward a globally educated populace living amongst the rapid developments of the Industrial Revolution, a new understanding took shape in the academic halls of Chicago and New York. A group of Unitarian students and professors in Chicago began looking beyond theism and sought a different path forward for humanity as a whole – one based purely in human behavior on an individual and mass scale. They formed the Humanist Fellowship in 1927.

The First Humanist Society of New York was summarily founded by Charles Francis Potter, a former Unitarian minister. In his book, *Humanism: A New Religion*, he espoused the values of rationalism, socialism, materialism, and naturalism while openly rejecting traditional Christian beliefs related to dependency on God, thus putting humanity's feet firmly on the ground and appointing them as responsible for their actions and their potential undoing. Crucially, humanism was recognized to be an ever-evolving understanding that could adapt to new knowledge rather than a rigid belief system, affirming humanity's ability to learn and grow.

The basic tenets of humanism were outlined a few years later in *A Humanist Manifesto*, a document written by 34 thought leaders. In it, humanity's place in nature is affirmed, along with the role of science and rationality in approaching any understanding of alternate realities or divine influence. Human activities, from science to labor to love and recreation, aren't meant to be divided as sacred or secular, but are instead viewed as methods of human expression capable of elevating their enactors to a universal truth and personal fulfillment.

Rather than focusing their efforts on worship and prayer, the humanist embodies their religious beliefs by leading their personal lives in a dignified way that supports social well-being. Voluntary cooperation joined with fostered intelligence are the twin engines that drive humanism toward its goal of a free and universal society.

Among the early adopters of modern humanism was Albert Einstein, who channeled his impressive intellect into writing on the nature of humanity and how modern knowledge afforded a new approach to the increasingly fragile human condition. With potentially world-ending technology now at play in the form of nuclear fission, the need to foster and apply a code of universal ethics became paramount.

Modern humanism was highly influential when it was developed, and it continues to be so today. Approximately one third of those in Western societies hold humanist beliefs, while a solid quarter consider themselves to be humanist. Humanist groups can be found in India, Africa, across Europe, and in America, continuing to spread the message of universal human capability, responsibility, and dignity.

Wiccan - 1950s

> *"An' it harm no one, do what thou wilt."* – The Wiccan Rede

As we near the end of our journey, we return to a primordial understanding of humanity's interconnection with nature. Such was the goal of the women of Britain who sought to unearth the traditional spiritual teachings of the region prior to the spread of Christianity.

Retired British servant Gerald Brosseau Gardner played a key role in the development of Wicca. Having traveled to Asia and gained a familiarity with indigenous spiritual practices, he also dove deep into Western mysticism, priming himself for a broad and inclusive understanding.

When Gardner returned to Britain in the 1930s, he found a group of women called the New Forest group practicing witchcraft in secret – a necessity given that Britain continued to maintain anti-witchcraft laws. Gardner learned from the group, transcribing their teachings. When the laws lifted in 1951, Gardner released *Witchcraft Today*, becoming a foundational text in early Wicca.

Followers of Wicca dedicate themselves to the worship of Nature, sometimes incorporating personification in the form of Mother Nature and Father Sky. Other deities may be included as focal points of worship, drawn from ancient pantheons (such as Diana, the Roman fertility goddess; Hecate, the Greek goddess of magic; and Aset or Isis, the Egyptian goddess of healing and magic) as well as contemporary religions around the world (such as Lilith, who was Adam's first wife but became rejected when she demanded equality).

Apart from identifying personally-chosen deities to offer their dedications to, Wiccans worship the turning of the seasons, particularly honoring solstices and equinoxes as sacred days. During these timeframes, Wiccans believe, the veil between the physical world and the spiritual world becomes thinner, enabling the spiritually-disciplined to connect with profound energy that can be directed into prayers (spells).

Today, there is no single text that is regarded as fundamental or scriptural in the Wiccan faith, leaving a significant amount of variety in how followers practice. In some cases, women – and men, who are regarded as equals in accordance with the ideals of feminism that helped fuel Wicca's rise – meet in covens, while in the majority of instances, Wicca is practiced by individuals.

Given the lack of centralization and sacred texts in the Wiccan religion, there can be some diversity in how it is ultimately practiced – but one rule remains highest without exception. That rule teaches Wiccans that they may do as they wish as long as they harm no others.

In some cases, the call to do no harm is bound into the threefold rule, which states that any harm done to someone else will come back to harm the instigator threefold.

Unitarian Universalist - 1961

> *"We affirm and promote respect for the interdependent web of all existence of which we are a part."* –
> Unitarian Universalism Principles

Universalism has a long history in America, finding its start with the Universalist Church of America in 1793. Just a few decades later, Unitarianism similarly launched in the new world with the American Unitarian Association. The two understandings remained separate and distinct until merging together as a new entity in 1961. With that, the Unitarian Universalist (UU) creed was born.

In accordance with UU teachings, followers learn best how to practice their faith by living their lives. Commonplace experiences, no matter how mundane they may seem, are worthy of careful reflection and introspection, with a goal of providing the supplicant with a greater understanding of interconnection and personal meaning. These experiences may be shared later with a group to help further shared wisdom.

Apart from valuing personal experience as the primary source of spiritual growth, UUs honor the teachings of all religions around the world, as exemplified by the Western Unitarian Conference of 1897 and the establishment of the World's Parliament of Religions in 1893. Religious teachings from Christianity to Hinduism to Shintoism and beyond are recognized as having merits that, when combined, create a greater, more nuanced understanding based on commonalities.

Because of the emphasis on personal experience, and considering the incorporation of all other faiths, there is not a set creed that UUs must abide by. Instead, UUs are joined by covenant alone, and that covenant can vary by congregation.

With that said, along with working to identify and exalt universal truths, UUs adhere to the core values of the separate faiths that originally comprised them, most of which are represented within the faith's seven principles. Of these, the most important is the adherence to the Beloved Community, a concept that dates back to the Massachusetts congregation of 1648.

In accordance with Universalism's teachings, UUs believe that humanity is saved only by embracing God's love – and, as the understanding evolved in the 19th century, that the Kingdom of Heaven is realized whenever we express and embody our love for one another.

The importance of caring for the marginalized is foremost in UU practice, as indicated by the participation of both Unitarians and Universalists in the Social Gospel movement that emerged in the U.S. in the 1870s. Similarly, UU congregations have been on the frontlines of equality battles for centuries, endeavoring to support humans around the world regardless of their race, gender, or orientation.

The UU perception of equality is not limited to humanity. The 7th and final principal of the UU faith is the recognition of the interdependence of all life, and the ensuing need to protect those sacred bonds by treating the natural world with as much dignity as humans are afforded. As such, it encompasses the concept of the oneness of existence.

Conclusion

It was the Irishman James Joyce who said we walk through life, day after day, meeting ourselves. The story of humanity is a similar one – regardless of where we go, regardless of the time passed, we find only ourselves, existing in one of myriad states of the human condition.

Looking deep into that self, peering into eyes simultaneously strange and familiar, what can we see? Just as the life of any one human is a unique kaleidoscope of experience, so too is that of any community or civilization. And yet, beyond all of the noise of color, a singular glow appears.

Whether from upon mountaintops or amid crowded city streets, spiritual leaders who have sought to know our existential truths have consistently found the same answer. In seeing our oneness, a philosophy of reciprocity becomes the only path forward for a just life. What we do to one another, we do to ourselves.

That's not to say the Golden Rule is perfect as an ethical philosophy. Detractors point out that to be fully reciprocal in benefit, the concept should be relativistic and thus closer to "do unto others what they feel is best for them, as you would have them do what you feel is best for you." After all, if I prefer sharp and concise instructions, and render them unto you – who prefer gentle and open-ended guidance – I have done a disservice to you.

In its simplest essence, however, the golden rule serves its function of intimating reciprocity, and in that, we find the ideals of egalitarianism, equality, and social responsibility.

When evaluating individual golden rules, it becomes clear that they differ in who they apply to based in the context of their origination. To some cultures, it's only male humans, while others include women. Other cultures encompass animals, plants, and all living things in their understanding. In its broadest interpretation, inorganic matter such as rocks and water are also included. In that sense, the Golden Rule leads to additional ideals such as animal welfare, environmentalism, and resource conservation.

Of course, the Golden Rule is rarely codified by governments, meaning the ideals that stem from it do not often make it into governmental policy (and, indeed, the opposite is often true). As such, governments are more likely to serve as the oppositional catalysts of the development of the Golden Rule rather than being the sources or champions of it.

Whenever it develops, the Golden Rule serves to remind us of our inherent connection to one another and the world around us. We learn from one another's actions, and in our actions, we teach those around us. The Hebrew word *abracadabra* means "I create what I speak." In this, we find our capacity for individual and collective magic rests in our ability to create our desired world.

As a whole, golden rules teach that holiness comes – again and again – not from any particular happenstance of place of birth, skin color, ancestry, resources, and so on, but from how we act toward one another. That is the constant. Treating one another with reciprocity is acting in universal holiness, and, as such, lends to the perpetuation of a bettering world.

Taken together, the golden rules are a beautiful example of plurogenesis, originating in multiple points around the world across time and rejoining in a raveling braid. This braid – whether whole or in parts – represents humanity's inner truth, our foundational spiritual essence, guiding us to and through the wonder and the challenge of shared existence.

Bibliography and additional resources

View sources and additional multimedia materials by scanning the above QR code with your phone's camera or going to www.lurajackson.com

Acknowledgements

My enduring gratitude belongs to humanity. Thank you for carrying your lives and your stories together, one step at a time, one day at a time. I know it isn't always easy. But you brought us to this moment. Thank you.

On a more personal note, I would like to thank everyone - and there have been many, in various ways - who have supported the unfurling of this book over the past decade.

Thank you especially to my partner, John, for helping me understand that people and relationships are worth it. In challenging ourselves, we can become who we want to be. Thank you, my Keoni.

Lastly, thank you to the authors of the texts and writings contained within this book. I am not an expert in any of the particular faiths or beliefs outlined here, and advise readers to pursue the source material for a more direct understanding of their intentions. That their wisdom endures is a blessing for all of us.

About the Author

Lura Jackson grew up on the rural northeastern coast of Maine. There she learned, with the help of her parents, a robust appreciation for nature and ecology. She carried that forward into a fascination with human history and cultures, culminating in an interdisciplinary master's degree from the University of Maine with a focus on peace and reconciliation. In her career as a journalist, she continues to meet – and learn from – people, places, and animals from all walks of life. Her other books include *Images of America: Eastport* and *Images of America: Calais*.

Made in the USA
Middletown, DE
04 May 2025